Stock Market Investing

Cardinal Rules for Passive Income

Copyright 2016- Brian StClair - All rights reserved.

This document is geared towards providing exact and reliable information in regards to the topic and issue covered. The publication is sold with the idea that the publisher is not required to render accounting, - From a Declaration of Principles which was accepted and approved equally by a Committee of the American Bar Association and a Committee of Publishers and Associations. Officially permitted, or otherwise, qualified services. If advice is necessary, legal or professional, a practiced individual in the profession should be ordered.

In no way is it legal to reproduce, duplicate, or transmit any part of this document in either electronic means or in printed format. Recording of this publication is strictly prohibited and any storage of this document is not allowed unless with written permission from the publisher. All rights reserved.

The information provided herein is stated to be truthful and consistent, in that any liability, in terms of inattention or otherwise, by any usage or abuse of any policies, processes, or directions contained within is the solitary and utter responsibility of the recipient reader. Under no circumstances will any legal responsibility or blame be held against the publisher for any reparation, damages, or monetary loss due to the information herein, either directly or indirectly.

Respective authors own all copyrights not held by the publisher.

Table of Contents

Introduction 5

Chapter 1: Look at the Bigger Picture 6

Chapter 2: Get Rid of the Bad Behavior 9

Chapter 3: Don't Follow Wrong Information .. 13

Chapter 4: Be Mindful of Your Timing 17

Chapter 5: Beware of Buying Cheap 22

Chapter 6: Have an Exit Strategy 26

Chapter 7: There is No Making up Losses 36

Conclusion 44

Introduction

Congratulations on purchasing *Stock Market Investing: Cardinal Rules for Passive Income,* and thank you for doing so. The stock market is an exciting area for investing that intimidates some but is highly rewarding for those that chose to participate and invest this way.

Making mistakes is a required part of learning. This book will take you through some of the cardinal rules of investing in the stock market. When these cardinal rules are broken they can result in problems for the investor. Monetary losses and frustration will ruin a beginner or intermediate investor's experiences. By backing out early you may be missing out on the long term gains. This book will help you to learn what some of these pitfalls can be and help you stay in the game.

Not all stocks are the same, neither are all trades. Learning about the mindset as well as the market are two strategies that will help make investing more successful. These two angles will also be addressed in this book.

Chapter 1:
Look at the Bigger Picture

Stock market investing and trading can be a great way to create a passive revenue stream, or an active one, depending on the degree of involvement. You can ride the highs and lows and if fifty percent of the time or greater you make out well, then you have done a good job.

Day trading however is quite tricky and if you are a beginner or even intermediate stock investor it requires time, money and technological resources and skills that only more experienced traders will have.

Standard stock investing however is a great way to build a passive income and accrue your wealth. This book will cover some ways to avoid some of the common pitfalls that will pose as problems for your plan to grow your wealth.

When buying and trading stocks, you cannot overlook the Big Picture. The bigger picture of buying and investing with stocks includes an in depth analysis that definitely requires doing your homework and determining (FROM Prior BOOK).

However, an often overlooked and underestimated strategy is to not just look at the earnings (quantitatively), but to evaluate the stock qualitatively. Analyzing the stocks in a more complex way is a great strategy but it will not give you the bigger picture of what is happening in the world that could impact your stock.

By looking environmentally at the larger overall picture, you can see trends, popularity, the value of brand name products and services, and real world usage. These are aspects that add to the value of your stock in a qualitative way.

When selecting and investing in stocks it is better to have different plans. Across different market positions, if you use a cookie cutter type strategy you will find yourself limited or possibly facing losses. You should adapt to the environment, but you will have to remain open to learning new strategies and continue your education on stock market investing and trading.

In the following chapters you will learn a few of the cardinal rules for staying out of trouble and minimizing losses, while maximizing profits in a bearish-bullish market environment.

As you know by now, stocks represent a portion of a company's assets and earnings. If there are a lot of shares, each will be worth less than if there were fewer. If you own many shares, or *hold* shares, of the stock in a certain company than you have more control of the company (control as in profits, sometimes in dividends, and less commonly, in voting rights and other privileges).

Stocks carry risks, and with the larger risks come the greater potential for higher earnings. With the same investment of money, one can place their funds in a low risk portfolio and do alright over time, by building a steady income. If the same person choses to place that money in a high risk portfolio, there is the same chance statistically of having profits and losses, but they will be much steeper and deeper. Even the lowest risk stocks on the average can reap a ten percent reward on the investment, which is much nicer than a standard savings account with virtually no interest.

The following chapters will provide further information about some of the risk areas that a beginner or intermediate stock investor will want to avoid or to mitigate. Each chapter describes a problem area for which strategies for smarter investing also will be suggested.

Chapter 2:
Get Rid of the Bad Behavior

Some of the worst things that new or intermediate investors can do is to look at successful investors who model bad habits. We will go through some of these habits below in hopes that they can be modified or avoided completely to ensure you have greater success than those who engage in them. Having a healthy mindset creates stability and also helps to drive well-informed decisions that are not based on emotions. Basically, there is not room for emotions in a financial numbers market. Here is a list of what to do/not do.

1. **Do not start off by sticking to one particular stock.**

    You need to cast off the emotions of being tied to a certain stock. The best investors may do well for a long while, and accrue considerable wealth, but every stock has its end, and the best investors also know when it is time to cash out. Emotionally, it is hard for some people to let go of the thought that a stock is something to ride out through thick and thin.

This is generally a good framework, and it keeps you from short-term sales, but even when a stock does well it also has its glory days and they will fade so get out while it is good. By selling your favorite stocks you can also think of it as investing the assets you have gained into something else. Nothing lasts forever, so you need to move and be flexible. Some people may choose to stay with a losing stock on the other hand. That is entirely a different factor!

You also want to avoid selling stocks when it is not the right time. This will be covered more, later. Selling either too soon or too late are other problems. Many people do this based on emotion as well, and not necessarily based on their actual performance.

2. Do not try to chase the stock if it loses

Some investors are gluttons for punishment and cannot accept the fact that a particular stock is a losing stock. They may try to chase the loss by coming back at a later time to repurchase the same company's stock. Some think of this as "I'll show you" type thinking; a semblance of punishment to the stock itself that demonstrates to the investor that they can and will beat the market this time.

Irrational thinking is a huge barrier to success in the market and it will catch up to you every time. Some call it mythological thinking. People have fantasy notions, distorted beliefs about why a stock works or did not work. None or little of that may be true. Allow the numbers and histories of the stock speak to you. As a beginner, you learned how to read and analyze stocks. Sometimes a refresher is needed, to stay objective and to avoid this fantasy thinking.

3. Do not hold onto dead weight.

Although a good rule of thumb is to forget anything you have sold there are times when you may want to revisit an old stock. If you are in a position where you are holding dead stock you will only see its value spin downwards and it will not come back up most likely, so selling it would be a good choice. However, some investors think that losses are due to bad timing and luck.

Some people delude themselves into thinking until they sell their failed stock they haven't really lost anything, and besides, it may return!! If it comes back then mentally it may seem that it was a wash, or a win. This is also irrational thinking. Additionally, wishing, hoping, thinking and praying that a stock revive itself will not make it a reality.

4. **If a stock you finally sold off had lost but then bounces back, forget it unless it has completely recovered and is super strong.**

   Not all stocks bounce back. Most of the major company's stocks that are reflected in stock market charts show a comeback that is evident in graphs. Smaller or lesser known companies do not always follow these trajectories and they may bottom out. This is often overlooked as well. The big guys tend to follow different patterns.

5. **If you do mess up it is best to own up to it and move on.**

Chapter 3:
Don't Follow Wrong Information

Buying stocks on bad or weak information is a dangerous place to position yourself. If you are acting on secret tips, rumors, or getting advice from anonymous people you are not helping yourself and you may be heading for rocking shores.

1. **Use accurate sources for information.**

    Blogs, articles, books, online courses taught or written by experienced traders are better ways to get information. There are also real brokerage firms who you can visit at their brick and mortar locations for tips, strategies and advice. Some online brokerage companies offer limited tips and advice or at least have access to some writing or online courses through their trading platforms/websites.

    There is plenty of room for making mistakes and losing funds from poorly acting stocks as well as gaining income on successful stocks. However, wrong information and bad advice can take a seemingly smart investor down in no time at all.

2. Beware of anonymous tips.

There are hundreds of people in the media every day who are giving warning about what stocks to ditch and sell, or what the hot stocks are of the day or week. Some of these may bode true but not all will and you need to be able to discern the difference for yourself. Since you are investing your money you do not want a stranger who is removed from your investments telling you "for sure" what the best things are to do with your funds.

Friends and family or co-workers my also call alarm to the best and the worst stocks of the day. What you can do is to not blindly follow, but to go and do research on the company and the stock itself. Read the charts you were taught as a beginner and look for the right indicators that lead you to believe it would be a strong investment. If the stock purchase doesn't seem to be good decision then steer clear.

3. Don't chase the news.

If you plan to look at the news in terms of factoring in to purchase or sell stocks you can make it part of a well-thought out and useful strategy. However, many people have a knee jerk reaction after hearing or reading news. Just remember that you are getting news in arears.

You will want to pay attention not merely to the news itself that will impact a stock positively or negatively, but pay attention to the effect that the news has on the fluctuations in pricing afterwards. Again, look at the data and do your research before making a decision based upon news that may be out of the financial context.

4. **Avoid internet fear mongers.**

One of the easiest ways people obtain low quality information is through chat rooms or forums online where beginners (a.k.a. amateurs) are advising others based on their narrow experiences of gains and losses.

Not only may the advice be inaccurate or have no merit, but you will never know the true intentions of the people in the rooms. Perhaps someone wants to stir up arousal, feed the rumor mill, or encourage the dumping of certain stocks.

You may be very tempted to see and hear what other newer investors are doing, but you are advised here to use great caution.

Chapter 4:
Be Mindful of Your Timing

The aspect of timing with stocks is everything, and nothing at the same time. There is some mythological thinking as described earlier in the section on bad behavior. That is something that the investor should always be mindful of. The idea of time being good or bad is an illusion as well, as nothing truly is in the investor's control. A good and logical investor will be looking for a well-informed judgement call as to whether it is a better time to buy, or sell, or hold. Here are a few tips about timing.

1. **Avoid purchasing stocks that are on a downward trend.**

    Buying downward-trending stocks is extremely common and also extremely dangerous. Investors who think that they should buy stocks that are spiraling downwards need to have a few facts correct in order to make out well. The stock will need to stop moving downwards at some point, and it will need to come back strong. Additionally, the investor would need to know when and by how much this will happen. The timing and the knowledge have to match in order for this to be a good decision. Most inexperienced investors think that they know when these variables are lined up.

2. Do not think that you can outsmart the timeline.

Some inexperienced investors also believe that buying a stock is not as a risky deal when it is at its low price because they may look into that stock's past performance and see what it has done. However, what the new investor does not realize is that there are reasons why the entire stock market is betting that the earnings for that company no longer have a good potential for profit for shareholders. Thinking that you know better than the rest of the stock market investors is probably not a logical way to go. It is not a competitive game against the beliefs of others. This has to do with objective fact and well-informed and speculative action.

Besides, if the investor is looking just at past lows and highs, what looked like a low last year, became this year's high perhaps, if the stock did well. New lows and highs are created each week and month. So if the decision to purchase at the "low" is made, it may not be reflecting the entire picture.

3. Do not add more funds if a stock is dropping.

Dollar cost averaging is adding funds to your position by adding more funds to your stocks at certain times, or doing so at times when the price has dropped. This is not always rational however. It is usually done independent of the price as well, as with specific amounts of funds in set *time* intervals. It could also be considered *scale trading* or *price-based* dollar cost averaging when done with specified amounts set by percent declines in the stock.

Some frown upon the latter, price-based or scale trading, dollar cost averaging. By practicing this you are adding money to a downward spinning stock, which is a losing position. Something is clearly happening when a stock takes a downward dive, so that should be your first warning sign. It can also be looked at as filling the gas tank of a dying car. It is wasteful and you will most likely lose in the end, in your hoping that the car will come alive one day.

When you participate in price-based dollar cost averaging, you essentially are siphoning all of your other capital to stocks that are about to tank. Since there are no stops o downwards declines, and if you had set a percentage at which it would kick in, you have an infinite number losses that you can take until you are bankrupt.

4. Study longer-term cycles

A good investor looks at the markets over the years, when they were bullish or bearish, and other indicators such as currency and interest rate fluctuations. There are also seasonal variables to the stock market. The first quarter of each year, as well as the New Year, spark growth in general. There is a saying (also called the Halloween indicator), "Sell in May, and go away." This refers to a strategy for stocks theorizing that there is stronger overall stock growth from November to April. The tech industry stocks do the opposite generally, but some find this old adage to be useful. Consider it another calendar tool that you can use if you use your observation and research and determine that it works for you.

5. You can forecast time trends.

Markets often become stuck in *sideways* trading ranges which is about seventy-five percent of these *hold periods*. In the remaining twenty-five percent of the time in hold periods they will trend higher or lower.

In looking at the charts for that stock you can look back at its past performance to see if it is behaving accordingly and make your decisions from there.

6. You can just sit.

Some investors just passively wait out all of the patterns and conditions that fall into place over time in order to earn their profits. You may want to look back five to fifteen years in the stock market to get a better idea of longer term investments and what they represent for your stocks. It may be a better move after all to reallocate some stocks at this point.

Chapter 5:
Beware of Buying Cheap

There is danger also in buying stocks cheap or buying stocks that appear cheap, buying stocks that are hard to sell, and buying stocks that have poor liquidity. These latter stocks and assets are considered to be illiquid, *as due to the loss in value, they* cannot easily be sold or turned into cash. *They are* also be hard to sell and to sell quickly because of a lack of or shortage of investors who would purchase the stock. There is also a problem with buying too often on margins, or credit.

1. A fallen share price is not always a good buy.

Some investors compare a stock with its 52-week high. Someone may look at the data and think that anything lower is a decent point at which to purchase the stock. Yet the investor may not know why the price fell. Incidents that affect the company or the trade overall contribute to a drop in pricing. However, the reasons (known or unknown) may not equate to it being a good time to purchase, nor that it will come up and gain strength.

You should look to its viability for future growth. Assuming it is a good buy since it is cheap is a very foresighted way to think and can be very risky to the newer investor.

2. Be cautious of the liquidity of stocks that you want to buy and sell.

If you can sell a stock without causing a significant price movement, meaning, the prices are somewhat equal, then it is liquid. Liquid markets have abundant and active sellers and buyers. Stocks can be turned into cash and traded without significant losses. Stocks that have less potential for being bought or sold, or that have few buyers are harder to liquidate. These are illiquid.

You do not want to hold onto illiquid stocks and you should avoid even buying them in the first place. Do your homework in advance. Determine if the stock is easy to sell or trade. In general, stock markets are generally more liquid than the *options* markets, but there are still many which are illiquid. Smaller stocks are also harder to liquidate. As a rule of thumb if you trade liquid stocks you will save yourself stress and costs. There are many liquid opportunities in the market.

3. Do not use too much margin.

When margins are used in stocks, it is essentially borrowing money to make purchases. Margins are the equivalent to using someone else's credit card, but where you are stuck with the debt and the interest. There are upsides and downsides to using margins. They can help magnify your gains if your stocks do well. You can potentially double your money or better and also pay the creditor back, and/or reinvest some of the gains earned on margins. Yet, it also can make your losses worse. You will have the stock share drop and lose the money plus still have the interest to pay until it is paid back.

You do not want to get stuck with a large debt in using someone else's money to purchase stocks and you find that they fail. You also have to maintain your stocks differently, with a heightened vigilance. Every small shift in price is a threat to not just the stock but your ability to pay back the margin. There is an extra pressure. Additionally the stock brokerage firms may sell your stock that is on margin when it sees losses coming. It may look like free money at first when using margins, but it definitely is not free money and it carries obligations as well.

Just as with any type of credit or credit card, you should not rely on margins. You should use them as little as possible, or not engage with using margins whatsoever. You can make this part of your investment strategy.

Margin investing can be used wisely. It also can be used to take advantage of larger pools of investment funds at fairly low interest rates, comparatively to other types of credit.

There is a way that some suggest to find a balance of lending and investing in the stock market. If you want a high return, an investor should opt to put more funds in the stock market than let's say bonds. With margin investing this increases the likelihood of returns. You are borrowing against the stocks and investing the gains into more stock, thereby increasing the initial borrow (if the strategy is successful). If the interest rates as low enough and the investor can handle the risk then this may be a good strategy to pursue. As interest rates move lower, Federal Reserve Bank is lowering the rates to promote things such as these investments into company stocks to boost the economy. It is much larger in scope but the bottom line is that you should use them with precaution.

Chapter 6:
Have an Exit Strategy

Many new stock investors make the mistake of jumping in head first, taking too much on, and/or panicking because they don't have an exit strategy. None of this fees safe, and it really is not. An exit plan should be created for each and every stock before you make that investment. This should be done at the beginning and should take into consideration what happens with profits and losses as well. There is an adage that goes "When you fail to plan, you plan to fail." This is so true in this context.

1. **Be careful of plunging.**

    Plunging is when an investor purchases too much at one time of a single stock and then as the stock increases or decreases, the investor feels the need to react. There are two situations with plunging that usually occur. Either the investor will end up selling (and thus losing a lot of the money that was dumped into that particular stock) if the price fell enough to cause that trigger for the investor, or the investor will make a profit that is good enough that it triggers the new investor to sell and take the cash.

In both situations there was a nearsightedness of the stock itself. The result of the plunging lessened potential gains with the quick profit and cash-out. On the other hand, plunging can result in mounting loses, when the dip in prices precipitates a quick sell as well. Once in a long while this technique can work if the increase in the stock picks up and keeps going. It might increase in value and not look back twice!

This strategy is very common but sounds contradictory to the concept of investing for a passive income stream. If there was an exit plan, the desperate measures to react may not have occurred. That is the problem with this strategy.

The lesson of this error is to diversify and not sink all of your funds into one large stock share.

2. **Dot not sell too soon.**

Selling stocks too soon, as noted above with plunging, can cut into potential gains on the stock increases. You are losing out on the potential which is infinite. Some say this is worse than losing money on a stock that may bottom out. You will never know what you may have gained.

Most new investors do not yet appreciate how a large stock gain can truly be realized. Having a stock do well or even double is good but perhaps over years it will substantially do well above the doubling. Doing market research and looking five to fifteen or twenty years at long-term stocks is a way to learn about this possibility and how it would appear if charted.

To create a truly passive income stream, you must be willing, in most cases to ride out the ebbs and flows and not to sell because you suddenly become afraid. The chapter that discussed behaviors spoke of the role that emotions play in decision making. Fear can cause a good investor to short change themselves, and to pull out sometimes too early. This defeats the purpose of investing the funds and allowing them to grow. With experience you will learn to better gauge when to pull out and sell and when to hold steady.

3. Reconsider the use of price objectives.

Price objectives are when you set a price at which you will sell your stock when it hits that mark. They are often represented as certain percentages or are expressed in terms of the value of the stock. Some find this to be undesirable strategy as well. To some it stresses that stocks that are overvalued may keep increasing and stocks that are cheaper may be declining.

The reason is that when the companies behind the stocks had quickly increasing earnings, the price of the stock would seem high in relation to what is being made at present earnings. Yet it is maybe only a few times wat the next year's profits would be, even if next year's earnings could actually ever be known. The trend of a stock itself, and its performance is a much more effective way to say when to sell. These calculations of the value are not so accurate.

You are cutting losses when you engage with a price setting strategy, which is not so bad. Yet you are also but also capping your profits. So why not just hold them at that point instead? You would be better off most likely. Price selling targets usually lead to shorting your potential. In effect you are capping your stock profits since you cannot take more because you have set the price in advance. Guessing how much a stock will move is not an exact science. If you limit them however, you are limiting your earnings.

Brokerage houses and writers need to provide tips for selling to their retail clients. Therefore, price objectives are easy and helpful, so they are very popular for this reason. The outcomes are not always necessarily good however.

4. Do not fail to cut any losses.

To newer investors, it may not be so obvious that when stocks trend downwards or sideways, they will continue most likely to go down further at some near point. This triggers a cycle that can be seen in the stock charts.

You will always have a certain amount of losing stock. Remember this is a percentage game as well. If a stock starts to bounce back it will take a while to do this and you will still not be making gains on it. Your job here is to protect your profits, limit your losses, and salvage the rest of your portfolio.

When you have a loser, many investors go against what they should do. They hope the stock will bounce back (and we also saw this in earlier chapters). This is a no-no. You can almost always guarantee that the stock will continue downward. Most new investors watch this happen and take greater losses.

There is the idea about the opportunity cost. This can be much larger than if there was just a loss on the stock itself. Funds that could have been freed and reallocated to other investments are lost when you hold onto a dying or dead stock. There is a missed opportunity. This is yet another cost that should be factored in.

Behaviorally, again, it may be hard for some new investors because they have made a judgement error and they want to make it right. They want to rove perhaps that they can get it back. Additionally, getting rid of the stock is defeat once it is sold, with this mentality. There is a common desire for some investors to hold onto any stock losers. The rest of the portfolio might look alright depending on how the winners are doing, but just remember that it would be potentially more profitable. Not having a definite exit plan is wasteful.

Another reality which is overlooked is that the worth of the stock is not that which for what it was paid, it is only what it is worth now at present. This is also where new investors get stuck.

An example of cutting losses short is having a stock that has a decent investment. Let's say $15,000. If the stock starts to drop to $12,000 you see it spinning downward further and then you are at $10,000. Waiting for it to bounce back may never happen or it would possibly take a long while. You can save yourself what the current value of the stock is (not what you bought it for) and sell now. Statistically speaking you have a better chance at reallocating your stocks to one that has an upward trend. Using these longer term statistics are the keys to successful trades. You could also reallocate the sale of those shares into a new stock that is seemingly doing well (and that you have researched well but quickly). Take the $10,000 and put it into something that you potentially could make up the loss from the first stock.

5. **Commit to your plan.**

Controlling your emotions is one key to success in the market, and this holds so true to staying with your exit plan (assuming that you had taken the advice and that you have one). The plan will keep your feet to the fire through thick and thin. Think of it as your guide map when you are lost.

You will be determining what the best way to exit is when your stocks are doing very well, and you are earning gains on your stocks. You also want to include what to do when stocks are falling, which was just covered in the section prior. You also should set timeframes for each of these so you are not waiting (or losing in either funds or opportunities).

6. Do not let the fear of selling early stop you.

Some investors worry that they are selling short and they have lingering regrets. While selling early can result in capping your profits, it also can be looked at in other ways. By selling and reallocation funds to new stock that are also doing well, you increase your chances of making more consistent profits elsewhere. You can break out of bad habits and look at new patterns and ways of thinking and doing.

7. Make sure you have a comprehensive plan.

As stated prior, your exit plan should apply to buying and selling. You should set in your plan a pre-determined number or percentage of gains that will be sufficient for you before you were to sell. Also include what you are willing to tolerate on the downside. Also factor in the time.

At the point at which you reach those pre-determined limits, sell and get out. Don't stick around and wait. You might not be as clear-headed in the moment as you were when you wrote your plan. Remember that emotionally fueled decisions are not usually level-headed ones. Do not include room for advice of others at this point.

It will fuel your emotions further. Amateur investors can be misled into making decisions that lead to abandoning productive positions and to stay with ones that are dying. By following advice of those who seem even to have good intentions and your wellbeing in mind, you are feeding into doubts that you are trying to override with the plan. A good plan is more about you emotionally than it is to set rules in place!

Going also on rumors or bad information such as what was described earlier in the book can be misleading. With emotions surging from a loss or a large gain, it is totally impossible to make a good decision. Your chances of making a successful decision are little to nothing, statistically in these situations.

You may not want to consider planning ahead when you first buy the stock. You are most likely filled with hope and potential (or possibly even greed, dare we say) when you make a new investment purchase. Do not hold off shaping the criteria on which you will buy or sell until you are in the moment and it is too late for planning. Then it will just be a reaction. For this reason, a sound exit plan should be done before purchasing a new stock.

Chapter 7:
There is No Making up Losses

This last section is dedicated to go more in depth into some concepts that were addressed in earlier sections. This has to do with "making-up" for losses when your stock is dropping or even tanking. Some of the many strategies investors develop in order to accomplish this idea are to average up, double down, get even, etc.

1. **Don't double up**

    As a stock trader, there is an adage that concerns making up for past losses by "doubling up to catch up". For example, if you bought a stock at a certain price and it falls, you may have the temptation to purchase more of the stock to lower the net cost and see something for it. It might work but it might not to double up. Doubling up by averaging down (see next section) may work. In this case you will double your profit or more when the stock bounces, purchasing it at a lower rate not than when you first purchased it but from what the price is now. You also may be severely compromising your risk tolerance this way.

When you are faced with drops in pricing you do not know how you will react in the moment. You should have a good plan if you recall, as well. You also may have the temptation to break your own rules so that you are able to keep on buying and selling the same stocks. Remember that the whole world out there cannot be wrong and there is a reason the stocks are declining.

You may find yourself in that moment of panic and asking if you would have done this when you first bought your stocks. You probably would not have even considered doubling up. You also probably do not have this in your planning strategies. So do not give in when the moment is heated.

Cut your losses, sell and close. You can redistribute your funds elsewhere and have an opportunity to see some consistent growth. "Doubling up" as a strategy does not always make sense. If you want to try it and find that it works, that is a decision your will need to make but be warned.

2. Don't make losses worse by averaging down.

Remember, a stock's performance in the present or future does not correlate to what you paid for the shares. You want to know the reasons for the change if you see them decline. Again, if it does not seem likely the stock will rebound, seek opportunities elsewhere. Close those stocks and reinvest what funds you have left.

No investors like to admit they have made a mistake. "Averaging down" means that you have bought a stock, it dropped in price and then you decided to buy more shares. It is pretty risky way to work and you could put your entire stock portfolio at risk. This is why you need a planned exit strategy.

Admitting that the stock in question is a losing investment is half of the battle. Thinking that you will buy more shares of the stock when it is cheaper may work if the stock bounces back but it is probably not likely.

If you insist on averaging down you should know a few things in order to make that decision. It should be used not as an all-purpose strategy but should be used in a select, one-on-one way. The analytics of the company/companies in question should be looked at before deciding to average down or double up. You will want to know if the decline looks to be surely a permanent one, or if it possible could be a temporary fluctuation. Is the company stable? The company's long-term earnings charts should be examined closely, their position for competition, etc. You can best implement a possible averaging down strategy with companies that have a low risk for bankruptcy, , debt free or low debts, a long-term record of doing well, a strong performance position that competes with others.

You can also look to variables such as management. A retiring or resigning director is always a factor in possible changes or disruptions to a company's performance at least in the short-term. Tech and blue chip stocks sometimes fit this pretty well.

Oddly, you are being instructed not to panic and act on rash decisions for doing things like averaging down. But if you stay level-headed, and have a plan for quickly assessing the factors above that will make averaging down seem likely or unlikely for you to do well it may be an option. The odd part of the advice you are about to receive is that when the market is not doing well and there is panic (from the stock market, not you), good quality stocks may be liquidated at great prices for you.

As recent historical examples, we had technology stocks were selling at ridiculously low prices in the early 2000's. Later that decade, U.S. national and international banks stocks dipped to low prices as well. Part of the conundrum at a time like this however is not whether to buy a low priced, high quality stock, but to know that statistically this stock will most likely bounce back and be strong.

Being a newer investor, you should follow a sound strategy for investing, ad have it be one that includes an exit plan. Do not rely on luck. This doesn't work for the stocks setting. Selling stocks and cutting your losses prevents before your losses from increasing. If you do not have a logical and well planned way to stay in the game at that moment and relative to that particular stock then you are gambling with your money more so than the stock market is already a gamble.

We also know that a stock will wax and wane as a normal process of price fluctuations of the market. Containing losses when there already dips is important across many strategies.

All in all, we have looked at a couple of strategies to maintain and hold your position, to create a position where by to sell or not to sell, and also how to mitigate your losses when needed.

Having a written investment strategy with an exit plan built in creates a framework and discipline for yourself. This plan and strategy should include the technical aspects of the research you will conduct as well as financial factors. Be sure to include both qualitative and quantitative data.

It will also help you to not have to work in a panic mode and decide at the last second if you should be doing things like averaging down and doubling up.

If you were to look back at all of your shares of stock that you have now you should try to ask yourself if you would buy then again if you knew then what you know now. If you do not like the answer then consider parting with it. Close it out and reinvest the funds elsewhere where you feel comfortable with your decision. You may have been missing on opportunities all along, so now is your time to explore some.

Most people will be able to tell you the strategy they used to purchase a new stock, but they may not be able to tell you why they are deciding to sell other than the stock was not doing well. You should have concrete reasons for selling stocks when these things occur. If you chose to use news or even a price target strategy at least you have one. That counts for something. The stop-loss orders that you can also set will help you limit losses. These kick in when the bottom limit you have set on your losses is triggered and you have set an instruction for the stock to sell at that point. This is a great strategy to mitigate damage done once a stock is in a downward trend. You have already pre-determined what you can or cannot live with and you have done it in a planning stage, not in a possibly irrational panic mode.

A *tax-loss harvesting* strategy is another way to mitigate losses. You may or may not know as a beginning investor that you receive tax credits with losses. Your tax credits can be used then to offset the taxes you will have on your possible gains. Knowing this and building in as part of your plan may help alter some behavior such as holding on to dipping stocks. It should encourage one to know that holding losing stocks not only increases the chances for further losses, it limits opportunities you may have had elsewhere and it also now affects the tax credits that you can use to offset capital gains. If there was one reason to not hold onto dead weight, you now have three.

You should always act before your losses deepen. You cannot avoid losing money entirely in the stock market, but you can take precautions and you can plan ahead wisely.

Conclusion

Thank for reading *Stock Market Investing: The Cardinal Rules for Passive Income.* I hope it was informative and that it will help you take the beginner's information that you have learned and take it to the next level. It is hoped that you will feel more comfortable putting yourself out there into the market and that you will begin to use smarter strategies.

The stock market innately creates large gains and losses as we all know. Therefore, as a result, there is no lack of opinion or advice that will follow a market as volatile as the stock market. In this book you will have received tips and rules that will help navigate the sea of advice and, quite frankly, poor information that will mislead you.

Being misled or making mistakes in the stock market however means a hit to your bank account. Some of us can withstand a small hit, and some of us can withstand larger hits, but this is not why we go into stock market investing. The intent of stock market investing is to have gains, and to generate gains which turn into cash and also assets.

There is still much to learn however, and once you are ready you can put some of these theories into practice. The tips and advice in this book should help to guide you as you face these decisions and obstacles. With more information you can make better and autonomous decisions. When you feel confident with you investment decisions your portfolio eventually will grow to reflect your thoughtful actions. This book is here to help you to create a passive income stream while thinking smarter and not working harder.

The other highlight of this book is the advice on how to create a strategic plan to invest. It is hoped that by the end of this book you have now learned why having a plan is so critically important. You also should know what types of things go into a plan to make it useful in high-stress or doubtful situations. Knowing when to buy, knowing when to sell, or hold, or to invest more can be extremely daunting on the newer investor. In this book you have read how to create this plan, what should be in the plan, and how and when to implement the plan.

You have also read about why you should keep your emotions as removed from the stock investing process as possible. Your human emotions can override any logic, statistics, world events, and theories as to why stocks are performing the ways that they are. The factors also should drive how and when you purchase stocks, sell stocks, or hold stocks. Human emotion and rash behaviors almost always intervene in a negative way.

The last lesson is to know when it is okay to leave. Again, human emotions may try to override rational decision making here as well. Leaving a stock, closing it out and never looking back is hard but it must be done at some points in every stock investor's life. The benefits of losing are winning in mitigating losses, increased opportunities in new areas, and tax credits that will offset losses.

There is not one right way to invest, and you will find many controversial viewpoints on these and just about every topic regarding stock investing. As with anything, you should do your own homework, do good research, and take guidance when you can.

Finally, if you found this book useful in anyway, a review on Amazon is always appreciated!

www.ingramcontent.com/pod-product-compliance
Lightning Source LLC
Chambersburg PA
CBHW070415190526
45169CB00003B/1271